Sounds of the Eternal
A Celtic Psalter

Morning & Night Prayer

John Philip Newell

Paintings by Tobi Kahn

New Beginnings
An imprint of Material Media, San Antonio, Texas

© 2012 John Philip Newell

Paintings © 2012 Tobi Kahn

First Published 2002 in the U.K. by
The Canterbury Press, Norwich

This edition published in 2012 in the U.S.A. by New Beginnings:
An Imprint of Material Media
San Antonio, Texas
www.MaterialMedia.net

ISBN 978-0-9819800-6-5

Design by Andréa Caillouet
Cover Painting by Tobi Kahn

Printed in China

To my dear friends
Elizabeth & Drew Cauthorn

My ideal world would be one in which
everyone had such friends.

Contents

Preface

In praying and studying within the tradition of Celtic spirituality over many years, I increasingly have been aware of the important place given to matter, whether that be the matter of creation, the matter of our human bodies, the matter of what we handle daily in our kitchens and workplaces or the matter of the body politic and how we handle the holy sovereignty of one another's nations and the natural resources of our lands. As Lord George MacLeod, the founder of the Iona Community in Scotland, used to say, "Matter matters, because at the heart of the physical is the spiritual." What we do to creation, therefore, what we do to our own and one another's bodies, what we do with the earth's resources is a spiritual issue.

I also have been struck by the similarities between Celtic spirituality and Jewish spirituality. Both traditions deeply honour creation, as my Jewish brother Tobi Kahn so beautifully expresses in the artwork that accompanies this new edition of *Sounds of the Eternal*. Perhaps I should not have been so surprised to find deep resonances between these two great streams of spirituality in that Jesus was a Jew, but we have tended to emphasize the differences rather than the common ground. In both traditions there is a radical affirmation of the goodness of creation and of the human body. In Jewish thought the body is the soul in its outward form. In Celtic thought the body is an echo of the soul. It is born and dies, and in that sense is passing like an echo, but it carries with it the sounds of the eternal.

In my publication, *Echo of the Soul: the Sacredness of the Human Body*, I draw on the writings both of Jewish mystics and of great Celtic teachers over the centuries. In both traditions the Genesis 1 description of humanity made in the image and likeness of God is the starting point for spirituality. It is the foundational definition of our souls and bodies, for the spiritual and material are conjoined. They are inseparably interwoven. In Kabbalistic thought in the Jewish tradition, the human body is like a sacred text in which we may discern the light of the soul. Within the body there are shinings of the eternal Self. The crown of the head is associated with the mystery of God's image within us, the centre of the forehead with eternal wisdom, the arms with strength, the heart with beauty, the genitals with creativity, the legs with eternity and the feet with presence. These are like the shinings of the true self to which we are being recalled.

This book is an attempt to utter in prayer what in *Echo of the Soul* I expressed in thought form. The theme of mystery, therefore, is woven into the prayers for the first day, as is the theme of wisdom into the second day, and so on throughout the seven days of the week. In the "Scripture and Meditation" sections for each morning and evening I have included brief phrases from Scripture that can be used as the basis for meditation. In both Jewish and Christian tradition the simple repetition of a biblical phrase, whether chanted or repeated in the silence of the heart, can lead us to what the Jewish mystics refer to as "one-pointed concentration", focusing on the presence of God at the heart of each moment.

Sounds of the Eternal: A Celtic Psalter is an expression of
the soul. Hopefully it gives voice not just to what is in my
soul but to the intuitions and yearnings that are common
to the human soul. The depths of who we are as human
beings share a birthplace in God. While we may cherish
our various rich religious inheritances, the essence of our
being cannot be contained by the boundaries of religious
definition. The soul is neither Jewish nor Christian,
neither Muslim nor Hindu. It defies the limitations of any
one tradition. As the 14th-century mystic Meister Eckhart
says, "the soul is naked of all things that bear names". My
hope for this book is that it might be used by Jews and
Christians, and indeed, by anyone who is seeking to be
renewed in the unity that is deeper than boundaries.

John Philip Newell
Edinburgh, September 2011

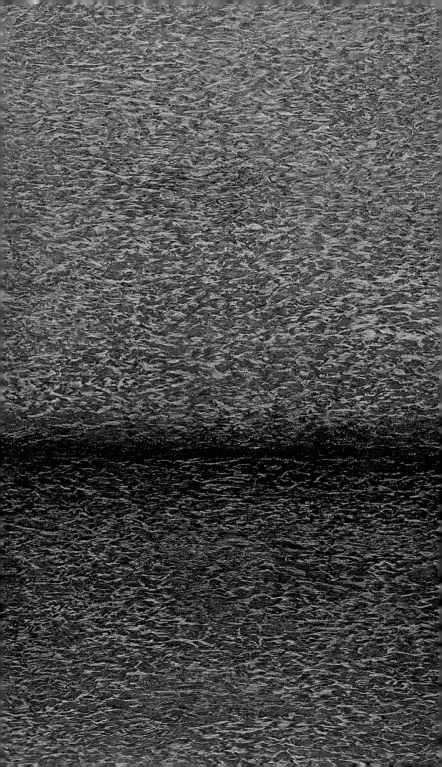

Sunday Morning Prayer

"Happy are those whose hearts do not condemn them,
and who have not given up hope."
—*Ecclesiasticus 14:2*

Silence
*Be still and aware of God's presence
within and all around*

Opening Prayer

You are above us, O God,
you are within.
You are in all things
yet contained by no thing.
Teach us to seek you in all that has life
that we may see you as the Light of life.
Teach us to search for you in our own depths
that we may find you in every living soul.

Scripture & Meditation

"For you alone, O God, my soul waits in silence,
for my hope is in you."
—*Psalm 62:5*

"Those who wait for God shall renew their strength."
—*Isaiah 40:31*

Prayers of Thanksgiving & Intercession

That you have made us in the image
    of your own mystery
thanks be to you, O God.
That in the soul of every human being
there are depths beyond naming
and heights greater than knowing
thanks be to you.
Grant us the grace of inner sight this day
that we may see you as the Self within all selves.
Grant us the grace of love this day
that amidst the pain and disfigurement of life
we may find the treasure that is unlocked by love,
that amidst the pain and disfigurement of our own life
we may know the richness that lies buried
    in the human soul.

Pray for the coming day
and for the life of the world

Closing Prayer

Before us in the planned shape of this day
we look for unexpected surgings of new life.
Around us in the people whom we know and love
we look for unopened gifts of promise.
Within us in the familiar sanctuary of our own soul
we look for shinings of the everlasting light.
Before us, around us, within us
we look for your life-giving mystery, O God,
before us, around us, within us.

Sunday Night Prayer

"In a dream, in a vision of the night,
when deep sleep falls on mortals,
while they slumber on their beds,
then God opens their ears."

—Job 33:15-16

Silence
Be still and aware of God's presence
within and all around

Opening Prayer

In the quiet of the night
may we know your presence, O God.
At the ending of the day
may our soul be alive to your nearness.
Amidst the tiredness that overcomes our body
and the tensions that linger in our mind,
amidst the uncertainties and fears
that haunt us in the darkness of the night,
let us know your presence, O God,
let our soul be alive to your nearness.

Scripture & Meditation

"It was you who took me from the womb
and kept me safe on my mother's breast."

—Psalm 22:9

"You love all things that exist
and hate nothing that you have made."

—Wisdom 11:24

Prayers of Thanksgiving & Intercession

Like light dappling through the leaves of a tree
and wind stirring its branches,
like birdsong sounding from the heights of an orchard
and the scent of blossom after rainfall,
so you dapple and sound in the human soul,
so you stir into motion all that lives.
Let your graces of healing flow this night,
for our soul is wounded
and there is brokenness in our life.
Let your graces of healing flow, dear God,
for those whom we love are in need this night
and there are agonies in the life of the world.
There are agonies in the life of the world, O my soul,
and those whom we love are in pain.

*Recall the events of the day and
pray for the life of the world*

Closing Prayer

Bless our body and soul this night
that we may be renewed in the forgetfulness of sleep.
Visit us in our dreams
that we may remember our birth in you.
Protect us with your angels of brightness, O God,
that we may awake to the freshness of the morning,
that we may awake to You as the new day's freshness.

Monday Morning Prayer

"Happy are those who meditate on wisdom
who reflect in their heart on her ways
and ponder her secrets."
—*Ecclesiasticus 14:20-21*

Silence
*Be still and aware of God's presence
within and all around*

Opening Prayer

In the silence of the morning
we are alive to the new day's light,
alert to the early stirrings of the wind
and the first sounds of the creatures.
In the silence of our heart
we hear the yearnings that are in us and the fears,
the hopes that rise from within
and the doubts that trouble our soul.
In the beginnings of this day, O God,
before night's stillness is lost to the day's busyness,
open to us the treasure of our inner being
that in the midst of this day's busyness
we may draw on wisdom.
Assure us again of our origins in you,
assure us again that our true depths are of you.

Scripture & Meditation

"Let me hear what you will speak
when I turn to you in my heart."
—*Psalm 85:8*

"The desire for wisdom leads to a kingdom."
—*Wisdom 6:20*

Prayers of Thanksgiving & Intercession

That truth has been inscribed into our heart
and into the heart of every human being,
there to be read and reverenced,
thanks be to you, O God.
That there are ways of seeing
and sensitivities of knowing
hidden deep in the palace of the soul,
waiting to be discovered,
ready to be set free,
thanks be to you.
Open our senses to wisdom's inner promptings
that we may give voice to what we hear in our soul
and be changed for the healing of the world,
that we may listen for truth in every living soul
and be changed for the well-being of the world.

Pray for the coming day
and for the life of the world

Closing Prayer

Like an infant's open-eyed wonder
and the insights of a wise grandmother,
like a young man's vision for justice
and the vitality that shines in a girl's face,
like tears that flow in a friend bereaved
and laughter in a lover's eyes,
you have given us ways of seeing, O God,
you have endowed us with sight like your own.
Let these be alive in us this day,
let these be alive in us.

Monday Night Prayer

"I prayed and understanding was given me,
I called on God and the spirit of wisdom came to me."
—*Wisdom 7:7*

Silence
*Be still and aware of God's presence
within and all around*

Opening Prayer

We seek your presence, O God,
not because we have managed to see clearly
or been true in all things this day,
not because we have succeeded in loving
or in reverencing those around us,
but because we want to see with clarity,
because we long to be true,
because we desire to love as we have been loved.
Renew our inner sight,
make fresh our longings to be true
and grant us the grace of loving this night
that we may end this day as we had hoped to live it,
that we may end this day restored
    to our deepest yearnings,
that we may end this day as we intend
    to live tomorrow,
as we intend to live tomorrow.

Scripture & Meditation

"Show me wisdom in my inner being."
—Psalm 51:6

"I will show you hidden things
that you have not known."
—Isaiah 48:6

Prayers of Thanksgiving & Intercession

For the wisdom that fashioned the universe
and can be read in the earth's dark depths
and in heaven's infinity of lights
thanks be to you, O God.
For the wisdom of teachers before us
and their words and imaginative seeing,
for the wisdom of those we have known
and their silence and humility of speech,
and for wisdom's wellspring in our own soul
and in the soul of every human being
from which ancient truths and new realisations
    spring forth
thanks be to you.
Let wisdom unfold in our heart and mind
and in the men and women of every nation.
Let us see the foundations for a new harmony
within us and between us,
the foundations for a recovered unity
with the earth and all its creatures,
for the ground of life is in you, O God,
the ground of all life is in you.

*Recall the events of the day and
pray for the life of the world*

Closing Prayer

In the great lights of the night sky
and its unbounded stretches of space
we glimpse the shinings of your presence, O God.
In the universe of our soul
and its boundless depths
we look for emanations of your light.
In the silence of sleep
and the dreams of the night
we watch for jewels of infinity.
In the silence of sleep
and the dreams of the night
we watch for the shinings of your presence.

Tuesday Morning Prayer

"You lift up the soul, O God, and make the eyes sparkle.
You give health and life and blessing."
—*Ecclesiasticus 34:20*

Silence
*Be still and aware of God's presence
within and all around*

Opening Prayer

As daylight breaks the darkness of night,
as the first movements of morning
    pierce the night's stillness,
so a new waking to life dawns within us,
so a fresh beginning opens.
In the early light of this day,
in the first actions of the morning,
let us be awake to life.
In our soul and in our seeing
let us be alive to the gift of this new day,
let us be fully alive.

Scripture & Meditation

"Awake, awake, put on your strength."
—Isaiah 52:1

"Maintain the right of the lowly,
rescue the weak and the needy."
—Psalm 82:3-4

Prayers of Thanksgiving & Intercession

Thanks be to you, O God,
for the stirrings of new life in us this day,
for rising from the dreams of the night
to a fresh flowing of energy,
for the vitality that awakened our body
and the desires that stir our soul.
Let us know the power for life that is in us,
the life-force that is in our senses
and the might that is in our heart.
Let us know you as the source of such force
and be wise to its true streams and false currents.
Let us serve love with our strength this day,
let us serve love with our strength.
In heart and mind and body this day
let us serve love.

Pray for the coming day
and for the life of the world

Closing Prayer

The strength of the rising sun,
the strength of the swelling sea,
the strength of the high mountains,
the strength of the fertile plains,
the strength of the everlasting river
flowing in us and through us this day,
the strength of the river of God
flowing in us and through us this day.

Tuesday Night Prayer

"Heed the counsel of your own heart,
and above all pray to the Most High
that you may be guided in the way of truth."
—*Ecclesiasticus 37:13, 15*

Silence
*Be still and aware of God's presence
within and all around*

Opening Prayer

At the ending of day,
in the darkness of night
we seek an inner assurance of your presence.
Our body is still
and our soul is silent
as we listen for the renewing springs of your Spirit
deep in the ground of our being
and in earth's quietness all around us.
Guide us to the wellsprings of health
in the landscape of our soul
and to the hidden reservoirs of strength
in the people and places of our life
that we may be made well this night,
that we may be made well.

Scripture & Meditation

"You are the stronghold of my life;
of whom shall I be afraid?"
—*Psalm 27:1*

"You endowed me with strength like your own."
—*Ecclesiasticus 17:3*

Prayers of Thanksgiving & Intercession

Thanks be to you, O God,
for the strong arm
of those who have given us shelter in our life,
who loved us from the womb
and carried us as children,
who guarded us like watchful angels
and wept when we were in pain.
Thanks be to you for the men and women
whose passion for the poor is undying,
whose prayer for the oppressed is tender,
whose defence of the wronged is fierce.
Grant us the strength to cry for justice,
to be patient for peace,
to be angry for love.
Grant us the grace of a strong soul, O God,
grant us the grace to be strong.

Recall the events of the day and
pray for the life of the world

Closing Prayer

It is in sleeping that our body is refreshed.
It is in letting go that our soul is revived.
It is in dying that we are born anew.
Bless to us our sleeping, O God,
bless to us our letting go,
bless to us our dying
that tonight we may enter your stillness,
that tomorrow we may awake renewed,
that in the end we may be fully alive to you.
Tonight, tomorrow and always, O God,
may we be truly alive to you.

Wednesday Morning Prayer

"Those who rise early to seek God will find blessing."
—*Ecclesiasticus 32:14*

Silence
Be still and aware of God's presence
within and all around

Opening Prayer

In the silence before time began,
in the quiet of the womb,
in the stillness of early morning
is your beauty.
At the heart of all creation,
at the birth of every creature,
at the centre of each moment
is your splendour.
Rekindle in us the sparks of your beauty
that we may be part of the splendour of this moment.
Rekindle in us the sparks of your beauty
that we may be part of the blazing splendour
that burns from the heart of this moment.

Scripture & Meditation

"Strength and beauty are in your sanctuary."
—*Psalm 96:6*

"You are the author of beauty."
—*Wisdom 13:3*

Prayers of Thanksgiving & Intercession

Glory be to you, O God,
for the rising of the sun,
for colour filling the skies
and for the whiteness of daylight.
Glory be to you
for creatures stirring forth from the night,
for plant forms stretching and unfolding,
for the stable earth and its ageless rocks.
Glory be to you
for the beauty of your image
waking in opening eyes,
lighting the human countenance.
Glory be to you. Glory be to you.
But where the glistening is lost sight of,
where life's colours are dulled
and the human soul grows hard,
we pray for grace this day,
we pray for your softening graces.

Pray for the coming day
and for the life of the world

Closing Prayer

That in the elements of earth, sea and sky
we may see your beauty,
that in wild winds, birdsong and silence
we may hear your beauty,
that in the body of another
   and the interminglings of relationship
we may touch your beauty,
that in the moisture of the earth
   and its flowering and fruiting
we may smell your beauty,
that in the flowing waters of springs and streams
we may taste your beauty,
these things we look for this day, O God,
these things we look for.

Wednesday Night Prayer

"My soul is satisfied as with a rich feast
when I meditate on you in the watches of the night."
—*Psalm 63:5-6*

Silence
*Be still and aware of God's presence
within and all around*

Opening Prayer

Our genesis is in you, O God,
our beginnings are in Eden,
our origins are those of every man and woman.
Forgive us the falseness of what we have become,
the ugliness and divisions of which we are a part.
Restore us to the truthfulness of our birth in you,
the heritage of all that has being.
Renew us this night in the genesis of our soul,
the beauty of Eden deep in each created thing.

Scripture & Meditation

"Create in me a clean heart, O God."
—Psalm 51:10

"I will make your wilderness like Eden,
your desert like the garden of delight."
—Isaiah 51:3

Prayers of Thanksgiving & Intercession

We have seen beauty of spirit
in a child disfigured by disease.
We have seen gentleness of soul
in a dying woman's calloused face.
We have seen a willingness to be merciful
in the life of a people who have been wronged.
Let these be remembered in our heart this night
as we seek a renewing of life.
Let these be remembered in our heart this night
as we seek a rebirthing in our depths,
as we seek new birthings in the world, O God,
new birthings of your Spirit in the world.

Recall the events of the day and
pray for the life of the world

Closing Prayer

In sleep may our body be rested.
In sleep may our soul be renewed.
In sleep may our dreams be carriers of truth
borne by the night's visting angels.
In sleep may we know you in love, O God,
in sleep may we be known by you,
the Lover of every living soul this night,
the Lover of our ever living soul.

Thursday Morning Prayer

"From the rising of the sun to its setting
the Mighty One speaks and summons the earth."
—*Psalm 50:1*

Silence
*Be still and aware of God's presence
within and all around*

Opening Prayer

With you is the source of life, O God.
You are the beginning of all that is.
From your life the fire of the rising sun
     streams forth.
You are the life-flow of creation's rivers,
the sap of blood in our veins,
earth's fecundity,
the fruiting of trees,
creatures' birthing,
the conception of new thought,
desire's origin.
All these are of you, O God,
and we are of you.
You are the morning's freshness.

Scripture & Meditation

"My soul thirsts for you, O God."
—Psalm 63:1

"You shall be like a watered garden,
like a deep spring whose waters never fail."
—Isaiah 58:11

Prayers of Thanksgiving & Intercession

That from our depth new life emerges
thanks be to you, O God.
That through our body
and the bodies of men and women everywhere
heaven's creativity is born on earth,
children of eternity are conceived in time
and everlasting bonds of tenderness
are forged amidst the hardness of life's struggles,
thanks be to you.
That in our soul
and the soul of every human being
sacred hopes are hidden,
longings for what has never been are heard
and visions for earth's peace and
    prosperity are glimpsed,
thanks be to you.
For those near to us who are in turmoil this day
and for every family in its brokenness,
for the woundedness of our own life
and for every creature that is suffering,
O God of all life, we pray.

Pray for the coming day
and for the life of the world

Closing Prayer

In the gift of this new day,
in the gift of the present moment,
in the gift of time and eternity intertwined
let us be grateful
let us be attentive
let us be open to what has never happened before,
in the gift of this new day,
in the gift of the present moment,
in the gift of time and eternity intertwined.

Thursday Night Prayer

"To those who repent God grants a return."
—*Ecclesiasticus 17:24*

Silence
*Be still and aware of God's presence
within and all around*

Opening Prayer

At the setting of the sun,
in the enveloping darkness of night,
at the interplay of hours
with sunlight giving way to moonlight,
we step from the day into the night
with a desire to be still,
and in being still
to turn to you, O God,
and in turning to you
to return to the creative depths of our soul.
At the setting of the sun,
in the darkness of the night
we turn to you.

Scripture & Meditation

"With you is the fountain of life"
—*Psalm 36:9*

"You have power over life and over death;
you set free the imprisoned soul."
—*Wisdom 16:13-14*

Prayers of Thanksgiving & Intercession

We have witnessed inspiration of spirit
in the voice of a woman,
in the colours of an artist,
in the prophetic vision of a leader,
in the most simple acts of daily kindness.
We have experienced creativity in our own soul,
in seeing things anew,
in unplanned utterances of wonder and passion,
in the most ordinary actions of tending and caring.
In the life of the world this night,
in every nation and among every people,
let there be fresh stirrings of your Spirit.
In our own soul and the soul of the world this night
let there be fresh stirrings
    of your mighty creating Spirit.

*Recall the events of the day and
pray for the life of the world*

Closing Prayer

As earth requires rest
and the seas need time to be replenished,
so in resting may we be made more alive,
so in stillness may our creativity be born anew.
Bless us in the night, O God,
that we may wake refreshed.
With your ministering messengers of sleep
bless us in the night.

Friday Morning Prayer

"You make the gateways of the morning
and the evening shout for joy."
—*Psalm 65:8*

Silence
*Be still and aware of God's presence
within and all around*

Opening Prayer

In the light of the high heavens
and the infinity of dawnings in space,
in the darkness of ocean depths
and the sea's ceaseless waves,
in the glistening of a creature's eyes
and the dark life-blood that ever flows,
in every emanation of creation's life
and the warmth that moves our bodies,
in the inner universe of the soul
and its everlasting foundations
your glory glows, O God.
In every shining of the world's inwardness
and the warmth that moves our everliving soul
your glory glows.

Scripture & Meditation

"I love the place where your glory abides."
—*Psalm 26:8*

"Your immortal spirit is in all things."
—*Wisdom 12:1*

Prayers of Thanksgiving & Intercession

For the life that was in the beginning
and is now
thanks be to you, O God.
For the life that is now
and will always be
thanks be to you.
For those who have gone before us
and the men and women of every nation,
for the vitality of children
and earth's life-forms still to be born
thanks be to you.
In this great river of life
that flows behind us and before us
let us know that we are carried by you.
In this great river of life
that flows around us and through us
let us know that we carry you
and can reverence you in all that has life.

Pray for the coming day
and for the life of the world

Closing Prayer

That your glory rises in the morning sun
and sparkles off flowing waters,
that the glory of the everlasting world
shines in this world
growing from the ground
and issuing forth in every creature,
that glory can be handled, seen and known
in the matter of earth and human relationship
and in the most ordinary matters of daily life,
assure us again this day, O God,
assure us again this day.

Friday Night Prayer

"The voice of God is over the waters,
the God of glory thunders.
The voice of God flashes forth flames of fire.
The voice of God shakes the wilderness,
and strips the forest bare;
and in the temple all say, 'Glory!' "
—*Psalm 29:3, 7-9*

Silence
*Be still and aware of God's presence
within and all around*

Opening Prayer

In the temple of our inner being,
in the temple of our body,
in the temple of earth, sea and sky,
in the great temple of the universe
we look for the light that was in the beginning,
the mighty fire that blazes still from the heart of life,
glowing in the whiteness of the moon,
glistening in night stars,
hidden in the black earth,
concealed in unknown depths of our soul.
In the darkness of the night,
in the shadows of our being, O God,
let us glimpse the eternal.
In both the light and the shadows of our being
let us glimpse the glow of the eternal.

Scripture & Meditation

"The whole earth is full of your glory."

—Isaiah 6:3

"You made me in the image of your own eternity."

—Wisdom 2:23

Prayers of Thanksgiving & Intercession

At the heart of life
and in its heights
glory shines.
Within creation
and beyond
glory has its source.
Guide us to the heart of life
that we may know its heights.
Lead us further within, O God,
that we may know you as beyond.
In the sufferings of our heart
and the brokenness of creation
open to us further
the doors of the eternal
that through the pain that is within us
and the struggles that are around us
we may be guided to you as the heart of life,
that through the pain that is within us
and the struggles that are around us
we may be guided to you as in and beyond
    all that has life.

*Recall the events of the day and
pray for the life of the world*

Closing Prayer

Bless us this night, O God,
and those whom we know and love.
Bless us this night, O God,
and those with whom we are not at peace.
Bless us this night, O God,
and every human family.
Bless us with deep sleep.
Bless us with dreams that will heal our soul.
Bless us with the night's silent messages of eternity
that we may be set free by love.
Bless us in the night, O God,
that we may be set free to love.

Saturday Morning Prayer

"Wait for God,
be strong and let your heart take courage,
wait for God."
—*Psalm 27:14*

Silence
*Be still and aware of God's presence
within and all around*

Opening Prayer

Early in the morning we seek your presence, O God,
not because you are ever absent from us
but because often we are absent from you
at the heart of each moment
where you forever dwell.
In the rising of the sun,
in the unfolding colour and shape of the morning
open our eyes to the mystery of this moment
that in every moment
we may know your life-giving presence.
Open our eyes to this moment
that in every moment
we may know you as the One who is always now.

Scripture & Meditation

"Seek God's presence continually."
—Psalm 105:4

"I am the first and I am the last.
Do not fear for I am with you."
—Isaiah 44:6,8

Prayers of Thanksgiving & Intercession

At the beginning of time and at the end
you are God and we bless you.
At our birth and in our dying,
in the opening of the day and at its close,
in our waking and our sleeping
you are God and we bless you.
You are the first and the last,
the giver of every gift,
the presence without whom
    there would be no present,
the life without whom there is no life.
Lead us to the heart of life's treasure
that we may be bearers of the gift.
Lead us to the heart of the present
that we may be sharers of your eternal presence.

Pray for the coming day
and for the life of the world

Closing Prayer

In the many details of this day
let us be fully alive.
In the handling of food
and the sharing of drink,
in the preparing of work
and the uttering of words,
in the meeting of friends
and the interminglings of relationship
let us be alive to each instant, O God,
let us be fully alive.

Saturday Night Prayer

"The crash of your thunder was in the whirlwind,
your lightnings lit up the world.
Your path was through the mighty waters,
yet your footprints were unseen."
—*Psalm 77:18-19*

Silence
*Be still and aware of God's presence
within and all around*

Opening Prayer

Unseeable
we have seen you this day
in the lights of the skies,
in the greening of the earth,
in flowing waters.
Untouchable
we have felt you this day
in the warmth of the sun,
in the wildness of wind,
in the touch of another.
In and beyond our senses,
in taste and touch and sound
your mystery has been made known.
At the ending of the day,
in the darkness of the night,
in and beyond our senses
let us know your presence, O God,
let us know your everlasting presence.

Scripture & Meditation

"As a deer longs for flowing streams,
so my soul longs for you, O God."

—*Psalm 42:1*

"The mountains may depart and the hills be removed,
but my steadfast love shall not depart from you."

—*Isaiah 54:10*

Prayers of Thanksgiving & Intercession

In our mother's womb
you knew us, O God.
In our father's birth
and in the birth of his father
were our beginnings.
At the inception of time
and even before time began
your love conceived of our being.
As you have known us
so may we come to know you.
As you prepared our birth
so may we make way for fresh birthings of your Spirit.
As you sowed all things in love
so may your love for all things be born in us,
so may your love be born again in us.

Recall the events of the day and
pray for the life of the world

Closing Prayer

The rhythm of life is yours, O God,
the changing of the seasons,
the busyness of the day and the night's stillness,
youth's energy and age's measured pace.
For daylight followed by hours of darkness,
for the time of letting go
and taking off the clothes of the day,
for the time of lying down
and being covered by the night's intimacy,
for the overlapping of the seen and the unseen,
heaven and earth,
flesh and angels,
body and spirit,
rest and dying and new life
all part of your rhythm, O God,
thanks be to you.

Appendix: Additional Prayers

Written by John Philip Newell for the
Companions of Casa del Sol

The Prayer of Jesus

The Song of Mary

The Blessings of Jesus

The Song of Simeon

The Prayer of Jesus
(a version of the Lord's Prayer based on Luke 11:2-5)

Ground of all being, Mother of life,
    Father of the universe.
May we know your presence here,
    seeking your will upon earth.
Grant all your creatures food for today
    and strength for our families.
Pardon our falseness as we forgive
    those who are untrue to us.
Do not forsake us in our need
    but lead us to new birth.
For the glory of life and the light of life,
    are yours forever.

Amen.

The Song of Mary
(a version of the Magnificat based on Luke 1:46-55)

My soul sings of you, O God.
My spirit delights in your Presence.

You have cherished my womanhood.
You have honoured earth's body.

All will know the sacredness of birth.
All will know the gift of life.

Your grace is to those who are open.
Your mercy to the humble in heart.

The dreams of the proud crumble.
The plans of the powerful fail.

You feed the hungry with goodness.
You deny the rich their greed.

The hopes of the poor are precious.
The birth pangs of creation are heard.

You have been faithful to the human family.
You are the seed of new beginnings.

My soul sings of you, O God.
My spirit delights in your Presence.

The Blessings of Jesus
(a version of the Beatitudes based on Matthew 5:3-10)

Blessed are those who know their need
for theirs is the grace of heaven.

Blessed are the humble
for they are close to the sacred earth.

Blessed are those who weep
for their tears will be wiped away.

Blessed are the forgiving
for they are free.

Blessed are those who hunger for earth's oneness
for they will be satisfied.

Blessed are the clear in heart
for they see the Living Presence.

Blessed are those who suffer for what is right
for theirs is the strength of heaven.

Blessed are the peacemakers
for they are born of God.

The Song of Simeon
(a version of the Song of Simeon based on Luke 2:29-32)

Life within all life, Soul behind all souls,
let me now depart in peace as you have promised.
For my eyes have seen the hope
revealed by you in the midst of all nations.
Light for the universe
and glory for earth's children.
Amen.

John Philip Newell

The Revd Dr John Philip Newell is a poet, peacemaker, and scholar. In 2011 he received the Contemplative Voices Award from the Shalem Institute in Washington DC. John Philip divides his time between Edinburgh with his family where he does most of his writing and the United States of America where he teaches and preaches across the nation. Formerly Warden of Iona Abbey in the Western Isles of Scotland, he is now Companion Theologian for the American Spirituality Center of Casa del Sol at Ghost Ranch in the high desert of New Mexico where he and his wife spend their summers. John Philip, the co-founder of Salva Terra: A Vision Towards Earth's Healing, is an ordained Church of Scotland minister with a passion for peace among the great wisdom traditions of humanity. His PhD is from the University of Edinburgh, and he is internationally acclaimed for his work in the field of Celtic spirituality, having authored over 15 books, including *Listening for the Heartbeat of God, Praying with the Earth*, and his most recent visionary work *A New Harmony: the Spirit, the Earth, & the Human Soul*. www.salvaterravision.org

Tobi Kahn

Paintings from the series *Sky and Water*, 2008
Acrylic on wood, 7.5" x 5" x 1" each

Tobi Kahn is a painter and sculptor whose work has been shown in over 40 solo exhibitions and over 60 museum and group shows since he was selected as one of nine artists to be included in the 1985 Guggenheim Museum exhibition, New Horizons in American Art. Works by Kahn are in major museum, corporate, and private collections.

For thirty years, Kahn has been steadfast in the pursuit of his distinct vision and persistent in his commitment to the redemptive possibilities of art. In paint, stone and bronze, he has explored the correspondence between the intimate and monumental. While his early works drew on the tradition of American Romantic landscape painting, his more recent pieces reflect his fascination with contemporary science, inspired by the micro-images of cell formations and satellite photography.

For twenty-five years, Kahn has been making miniature sacred spaces he calls "shrines." The first full-scale shrine, Shalev, is in New Harmony, Indiana, commissioned as an outdoor sculpture for Jane Owen and the Robert Lee Blaffer Trust.

Among the awards that Kahn has received are the Outstanding Alumni Achievement Award from Pratt Institute in 2000; the Cultural Achievement Award for the Visual Arts from the National Foundation of Jewish Culture in 2004; and an Honorary Doctorate from the Jewish Theological Seminary in 2007 for his work as an artist and educator.

Kahn also communicates his vision through his passion for teaching. For 28 years, he has taught fine arts workshops at the School of Visual Arts in New York City. He also designed the art curriculum for several high schools in the New York area. He is co-founder and facilitator for the Artists' Beit Midrash at the Skirball Center of Temple Emanu-El. Kahn lectures extensively at universities and public forums internationally on the importance of visual language and art as healing.